PAPER BOATS!

Origami Boats, Ships, Yachts and Liners,
Ready to Float Upon the High Seas!

Carmel D. Morris

Preface

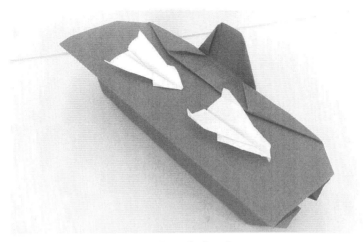

Aircraft Carrier

Welcome to a whole new world of paper folding for the high seas. If you like origami but find it difficult to make the more complicated models, this book covers all bases; from simple to moderately complex, although most models are easy to fold, many are fold-only, and to make it easier, the author is happy to use the occasional scissor snip to get the job done, so there is a model and skill level for everyone in the family.

So grab a sheet of colored paper, wax paper or waterproof chocolate wrapper and start folding. You'll amaze your buddies with your newfound shipwright skills.

Happy folding and bon voyage!

Dwight Edwards

Important note to folders

It is very important to practice all the basic steps before starting on the models themselves. Try the reverse folds, rabbit ear fold, plus the other folds several times before starting.

By following the symbols, folding guides and instructions in this book, your boats are sure to be more realistic when finished.

Contents

Introduction

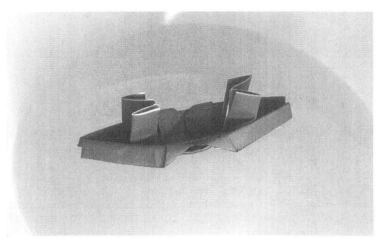

Ocean Liner

Ahoy there, me little sea captains! For thousands of years people have crossed the waters of the globe in craft of all shapes and sizes, kayaks and canoes, galleys and galleons, sailing ships and steamers, fishing boats and rowing boats, plus luxurious passenger craft.

Stories of romance and adventure on the high seas abound. There are tales of the Vikings who traded and plundered, of the Spaniards who sailed the galleons in search of treasure and lands to conquer; of intrepid explorers in search of new worlds, and villainous pirates who struck fear into the heart of many a sailor.

If you are an aspiring seafarer, if you love the feel of the wind in your hair and salt spray on your face, or if you just love mucking about in boats, then welcome to the fun world of paper watercraft. With the models shown in this book, you will be able to create your own nautical adventures on boating ponds, local streams, rivers, rapids, the beach, or even the high seas… in your bathtub.

These models are easy to make, even the clumsiest deckhands will be whittling their own paper watercraft to perfection and will 'learn the ropes' in no time. I encourage you to invent your own craft too since anything is possible with paper, or plastic sheeting for more permanent water use.

The Shipwright Stuff

Believe it or not, this book will elucidate you to some pretty nifty geometry as used in shipbuilding. Once you have mastered the paper boats, you may like to try your hand at cardboard or wooden craft. The shapes are the same, only the material differs. It's quite possible to make a life-sized version of a boat in this book. People have done it already (I recall as a child reading about a man who made a full-sized Origami rowboat out of newspaper that actually floated).

Inches and millimeters are used in various places throughout this book, so have a ruler handy that has both metric and imperial measurements.

Finally, read the instructions carefully and practice the folds shown at the front of this book before you start. Once you have mastered the basic steps, you won't be left high and dry.

Types of material to use

Models in this book are made from square paper or Letter/A4, but the size is up to you. I suggest you also try larger sheets of paper such as A3 or sheet card. Multi-colored waterproof wrapping paper would be ideal for boats on long voyages.

Paper must be crisp, not too heavy and be able to retain a fold without 'falling open'. For waterproofing paper, try lacquer spray on your model when it is completed.

Aircraft carriers are more suited to a metallic look and aluminum foil is ideal. However, aluminum cooking wrap is too thin so you would need to reinforce it with paper underneath. Use spray adhesive to stick a sheet of aluminum foil to a sheet of paper; that way the boat will be easy to fold.

Acetate, that is, plastic sheets as used in some inkjet and laser printers is ideal for making a boat you wish to keep. Provided the plastic is not too thick, it should be easy to fold. Note that when folding, some plastics retain the fold, especially if well creased. This is known as 'plastic memory'; therefore make sure your folds are correct the first time round, otherwise you will have to start again with a new sheet of plastic.

Remember to respect the environment, it is suggested to first only practice with old paper found around the house, such as junk mail. When you've finished with your model, don't throw it out. Give it to a friend, or make a paper boat mobile for the younger ones (if you have any in your family) or play racing games in the swimming pool, bathtub etc.

Folding Symbols

Models in this book use the following symbols.

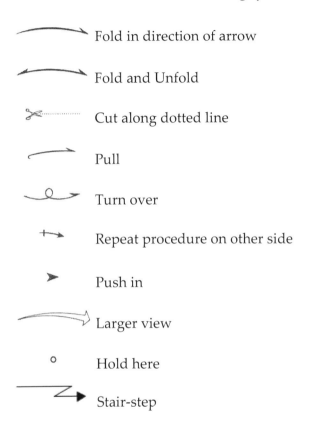

Fold in direction of arrow

Fold and Unfold

Cut along dotted line

Pull

Turn over

Repeat procedure on other side

Push in

Larger view

Hold here

Stair-step

Folding Techniques

Find some small pieces of paper to get your folding practice to perfection, and follow the directions shown below.

Valley Fold

This is indicated with a line of dashes.

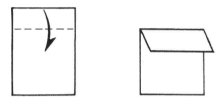

Crease Fold

Valley-folded over and then unfolded to make the thin solid crease line as shown in the right-hand image.

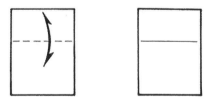

Mountain Fold

Folded behind and indicated by a line of dots and dashes.

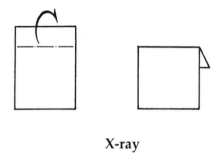

X-ray

X-ray or hidden view is indicated by a dotted line.

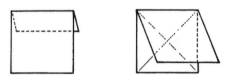

Push in

This is typically a double-mountain fold pushed into a paper model. Quadruple folds occur for pushing in the pointed end of a model consisting of four sides.

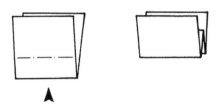

Stair Step

This is a valley and mountain fold, or a mountain and valley fold, i.e., a reverse stair-step. One can stair-step fold 'behind' or 'in front'.

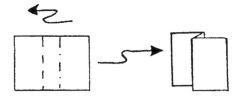

Rabbit Ear Fold

Step 1

Fold top-left corner diagonally across to meet the right-hand side and then unfold. Now fold edge to meet new crease.

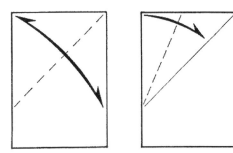

Step 2

Unfold and then fold top edge down and back.

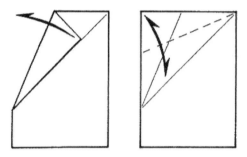

Step 3

Bring the sides together and pinch the corners to make the 'ear', and then flatten.

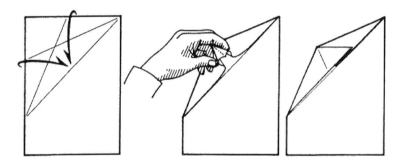

Inside Reverse Fold

This is where a point is folded at any degree inside,
turning the fold 'outside in'.

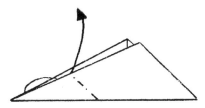

Outside Reverse Fold

This is where a point is folded at any degree outside,
turning the fold 'inside out'.

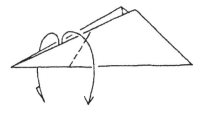

Canoe

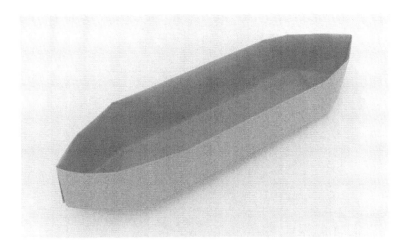

Now you can have your very own 'dugout'. If you make a huge version it could look like a tanker, especially if you fold a few boxes to place inside to look like cargo.

Canoe step 1

Using Letter or A4 paper, fold lengthwise in half.

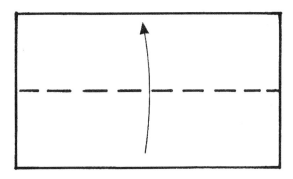

Canoe step 2

Fold the corners by an inch or so.

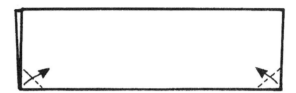

Canoe step 3

Fold the top flap down so that it partially covers the folded corners.

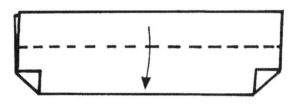

Canoe step 4

It should look like this. Turn the paper over.

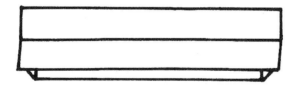

Canoe step 5

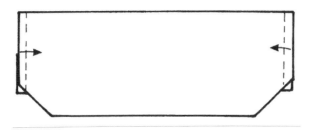

Canoe step 6

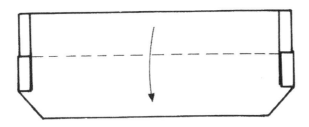

Canoe step 7

Crease-well the hull area, and then hold sides and pull to open out.

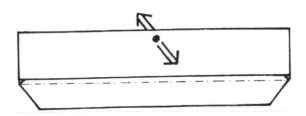

Canoe step 8

Almost there, with model upside down, push in the ends
where they jut out. Squash and flatten the fold to the
underside and then turn the boat back over.

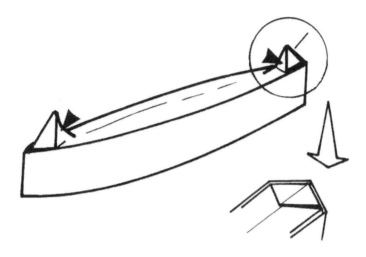

Your canoe is complete. If you're at a pool party, float one
of these to a friend. Make sure you fill it with candy first!

Gondola

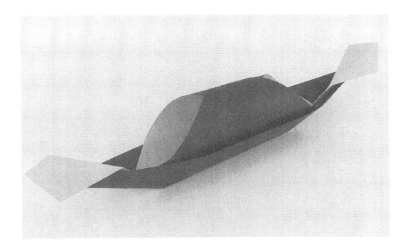

If you live in Venice, you'd be catching one of these (also known as a *traghetti*) to school. This model has the traditional 'felze', or center cabin. Although not quite a flat bottomed boat, you could with some push-in techniques create your own flat bottom so try experimenting; Tramontin would be proud of your boat-building skills!

Gondola step 1

Use a square of black paper (since traditionally, Gondolas are painted black). Crease-fold the paper diagonally in half, then fold point 'A' down, and then fold up along the half-way crease. Repeat for the other side.

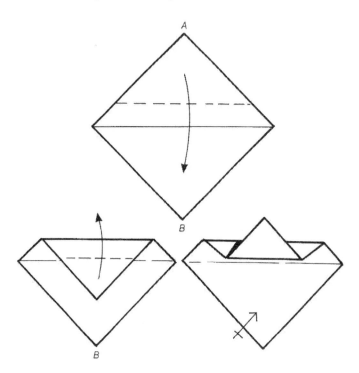

Gondola step 2

Fold behind the corners to lock the triangle sections. 'A' and opposing triangle will form the cabin.

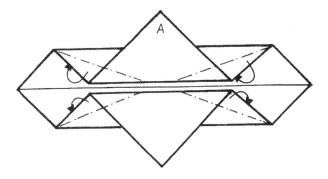

Gondola step 3

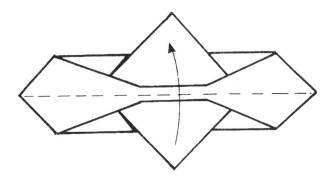

Gondola step 4

Crease-well and turn the folds inside out by pushing in the bottom edges.

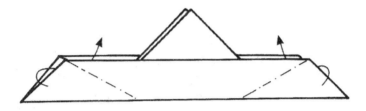

Gondola step 5

Crease the triangle sections on each end and flatten out while holding areas marked 'X'. Now curve the center triangles to make the cabin.

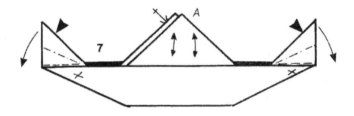

Gondola step 6

Cabin section shown; either cut a slit into one triangle section and slot the point of the other into it, or simply use tape to hold the two sections together to make the cabin.

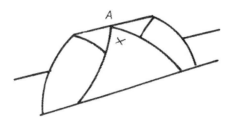

Your completed Gondola; you may need to add some center weight for ballast should it tip to one side. A coin would work; otherwise experiment by folding a quarter inch up from the bottom of the boat and pushing in and flattening the bottom.

Row Boat

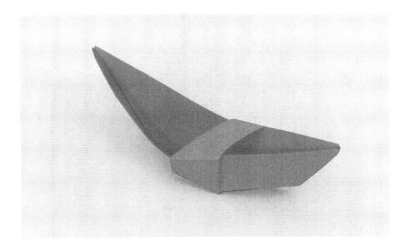

A simple craft with a seat; row boats go all the way back to galleys in ancient times where many rowers would be busy keeping their much larger craft moving. Row boats were more maneuverable than sailing craft and many ancient designs persisted over the centuries.

Row boat step 1

Cut a Letter or A4 sheet in half lengthwise and using one half, fold the right end across by one third.

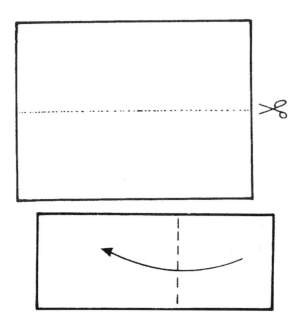

Row boat step 2

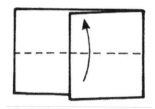

Row boat step 3

Fold upper edge down so that there is about a quarter inch remaining below, and repeat for the other side.

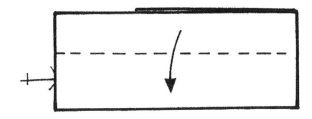

Row boat step 4

Make a diagonal crease-fold at 45 degrees on both sides.

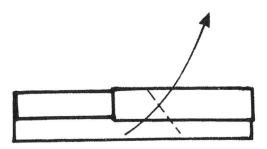

Row boat step 5

Unfold the diagonal and open the model out. Noting the creases, lift up the upper flap. Push in where shown and then collapse the fold.

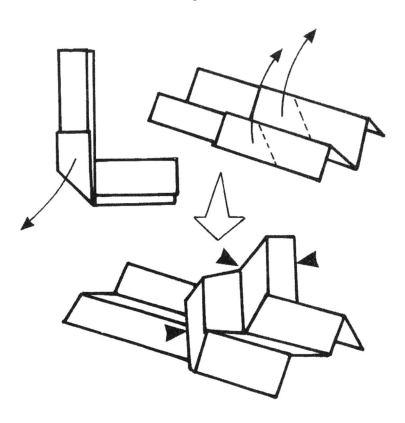

Row boat step 6

For the upper flaps on each end, and then fold bow and stern corner diagonals behind. Tuck the diagonals on the lower folds under the upper fold.

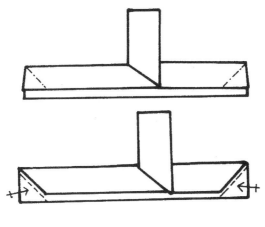

Row boat step 7

Fold behind outer bow flaps at new angle, and tuck in to lock the bow section.

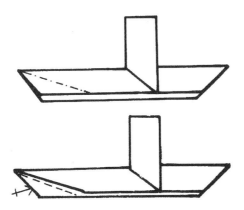

Row boat step 8

Open out the model and swing down the 'sail' section to make the seat.

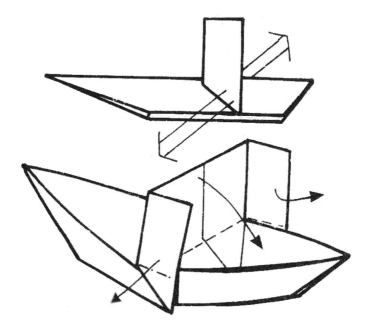

Row boat step 9

Looking down on your craft, fold the sides down and
against the hull. Tuck the jutting corners on both sides
behind the flaps underneath to secure the seat.

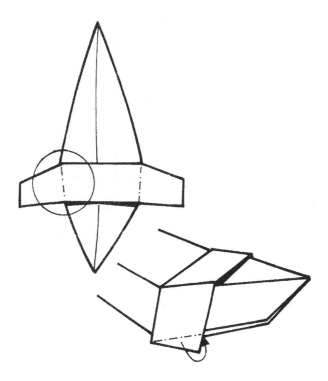

Your finished rowboat; this craft will float well and is very stable.

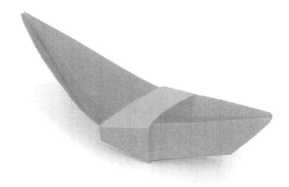

Speedboat

Looking a bit like a Spencer runabout, this craft obviously won't be able to go as fast but if you're at a pool party, and have make your boat in plastic wrapper, add some string to the bow of this beast and it should be able to take some pressure as you pull it across the pool. Try having a race with your friends in choppy water!

Speedboat step 1

The folding procedure is similar to the Rowboat. Use a sheet of Letter or A4 cut lengthwise in half, fold one end in half to meet the bottom edge of the other end and then fold the bottom edge of the upper flap up by about one-sixth.

Once you have done this, fold the model in half (bottom right image).

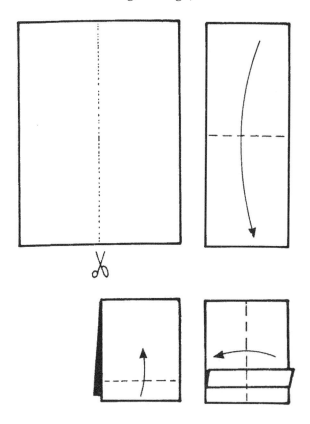

Speedboat step 2

Have the model facing you horizontally. Fold both sides down and then (lower image), grip where circled and pull up the center section by about 30 degrees. This will be our 'windshield'.

Lifting the section may be a bit tricky, so patience is required; the entire flap must be angled upwards so you would need to open out the boat a bit to raise the center fold.

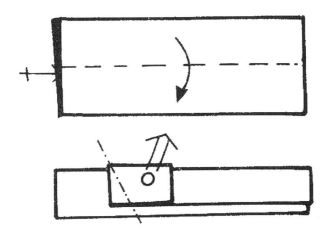

Speedboat step 3

Fold corners in as for rowboat to make bow and stern, and
then fold the center flaps behind to secure the windshield.
The lowermost image is an enlarged view; tuck the flaps in
to lock the windshield and then gently pull out the boat
sides.

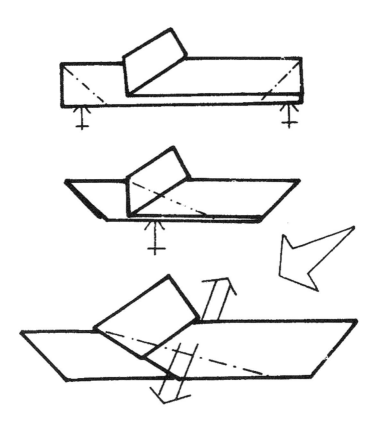

Speedboat step 4

Fold back the upper edge of the windshield and crease where indicated (though you may not need to do this depending on how well you creased your folds when making the windshield).

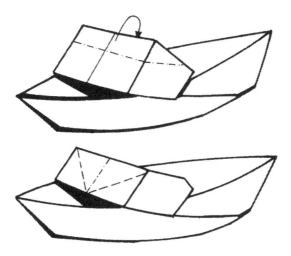

Your finished speedboat; ready to race on the swimming pool, bathtub, storm water drain etc.

Sailing Boat

This is more like a sailing skiff, a kind of dinghy with a sail. Simple in design, ideal for fishing (should you make a big one, to catch a big one) and very relaxing; or you could race with your buddies in the swimming pool and blow your paper boats till your lungs are empty (or cheat and use a battery fan). Whatever floats your boat!

Sailing boat step 1

Similar to the row boat, use one half of Letter or A4 paper
cut in two, and then fold in half.

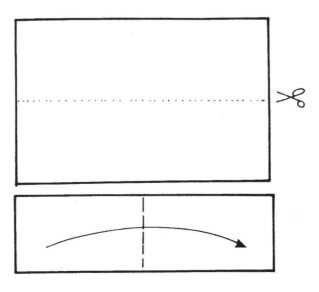

Sailing boat step 2

Fold the edges of the upper flap towards each other,
pushing in the left corners and flattening the fold.

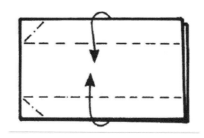

Sailing boat step 3

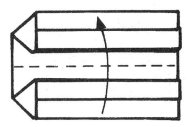

Sailing boat step 4

This image shows an enlarged view. Fold top edge down and repeat on other side.

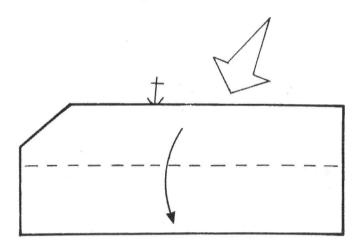

Sailing boat step 5

Crease-fold at a 45 degree angle on both sides and fold outer section up, and then flatten the fold.

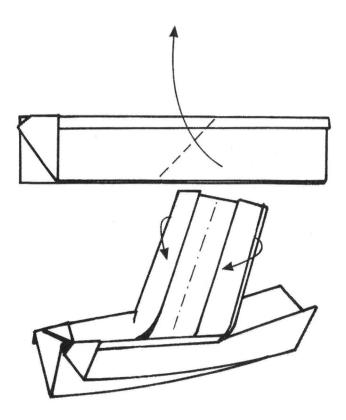

Sailing boat step 6

Fold the bow and stern as for the row boat and open out
the sail section, flattening the sail and creasing the sail
edges for reinforcement.

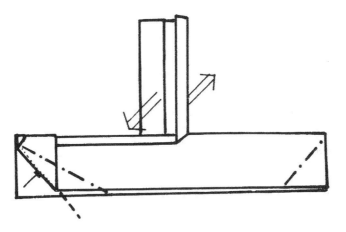

Sailing boat step 7

This step shows step 6 almost complete; the outer sail edges fold backwards and the center sail section is made flat to complete the sail.

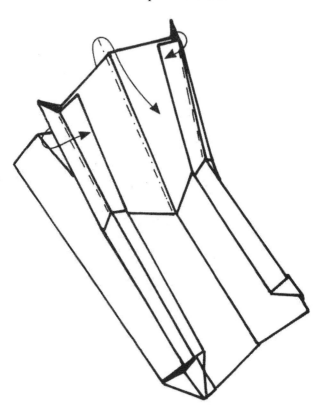

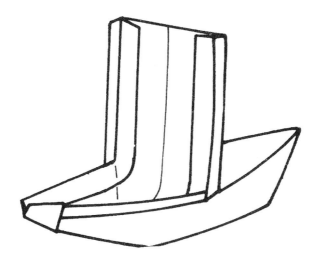

Your finished sailboat; take a deep breath and puff your
lungs out to sail this across the bathtub!

Folding experiment:

Using a much longer piece of paper, it's possible to fold this craft so that it has two sails. I'll let you work out how!

Two-in-one Yacht

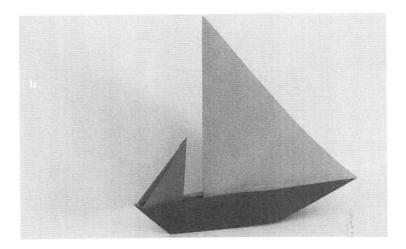

Although not shown in the image above, this is a yacht that has a jib which doubles as a small catamaran! The jib can also be used as a keel to keep your yacht stable in rougher seas.

Two-in-one yacht step 1

Make a square piece of paper and then make a rabbit ear fold on one side of the diagonal crease. Please keep the cut-off section for the separate catamaran.

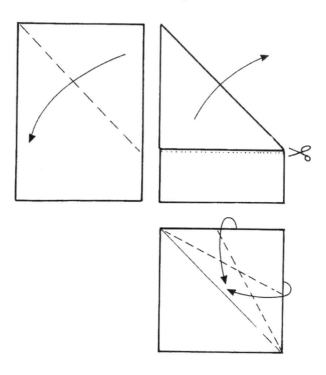

Two-in-one yacht step 2

Mountain-fold in half and then (lower image) crease-fold
well on the hull section.

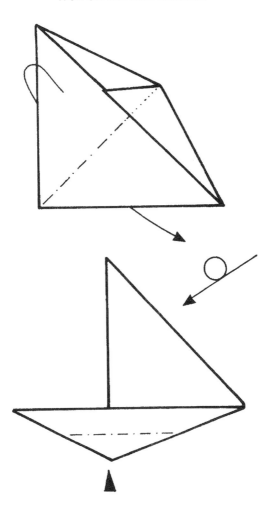

Two-in-one yacht step 3

Where you crease-folded the hull, hold model upside down, open out the fold and push in the center point to 'sink' it inside. You should now have an aft-sail boat as shown in the lower image. Put this aside while we start the catamaran section.

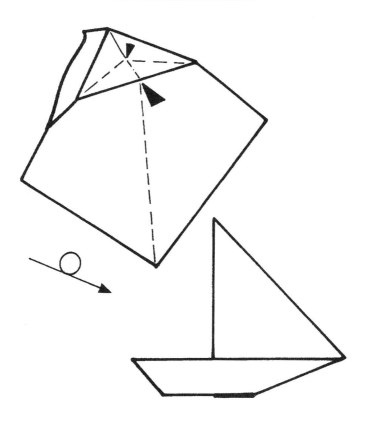

Two-in-one yacht step 4 – Catamaran section

Find the cut-off piece of paper you made earlier and make
what is called a 'water bomb base'. Make diagonal folds,
and one horizontal fold behind. Bring the sides together
and you have what is shown in the right-hand image.
Once done, fold bottom end up.

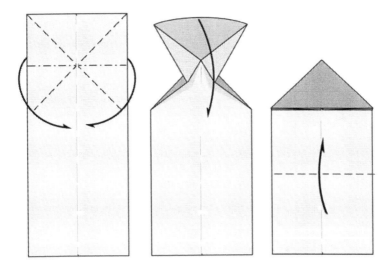

Two-in-one yacht step 5 – Catamaran section

Crease well and push in the section, similar to what you did in step 3. The bottom image shows the fold flattened.

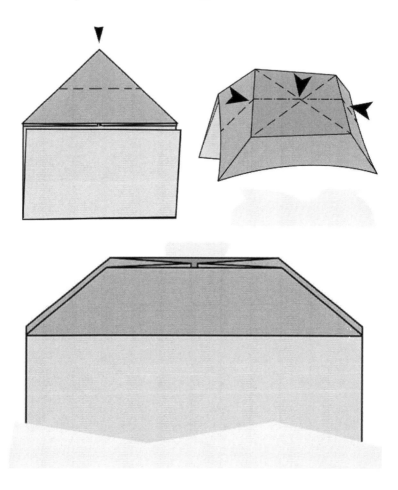

Two-in-one yacht step 6 – Catamaran section

Have the model facing you as shown and fold the back flap 'C' behind to meet 'B', leaving the upper fold intact.

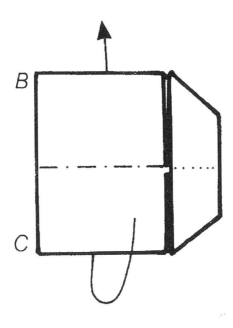

Two-in-one yacht step 7 – Catamaran section

Fold corners 'C' and 'B' in to shape the sail and swing
about to have your little Catamaran ready sailing.

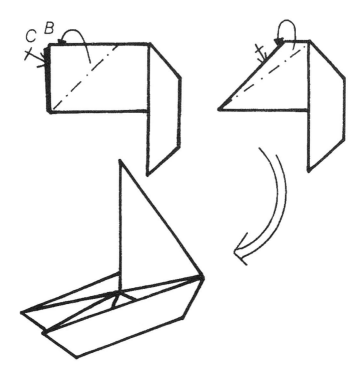

Two-in-one yacht step 8 – Options

Your craft is nearly done. This image shows the options.

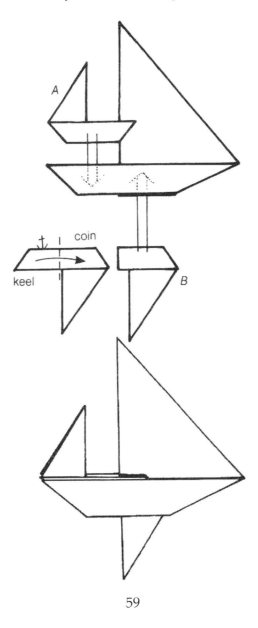

To add a jib on your main sailboat, slot the catamaran section into the larger sail boat's bow and hold in place with a small piece of tape.

Alternatively, make a keel by folding the catamaran bow to the right (note orientation 'B' shown), adding a coin for ballast and slipping up under and inside the main sailboat's hull.

Do both of the preceding suggestions for a complete sailboat! Curve open the hull a little to ensure it will float.

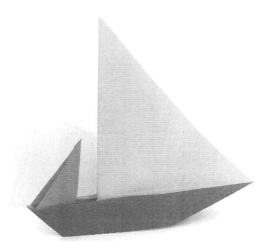

Easy Catamaran

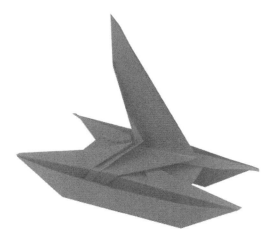

This is a very simple craft that moves well with good breezes. Try experimenting with the sail section to improve the capture of breezes. Try out different versions and race with your friends.

Easy catamaran step 1

Make a square, make diagonal folds on the square and
then fold the sides in to meet the center crease. Don't
forget to keep the cut-off piece - we'll need it for the sail!

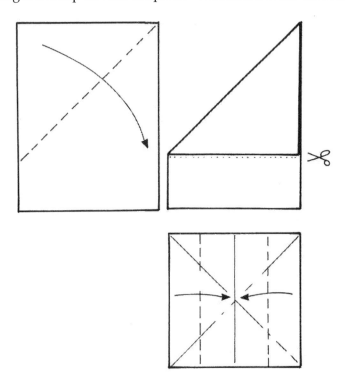

Easy catamaran step 2

Fold the paper behind in half and, observing the larger view (right-hand image); fold the lower edges up in the approximate area shown.

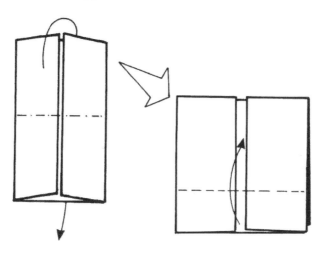

Easy catamaran step 3

Pull out the sides, forming the hull section, and then repeat for the other side.

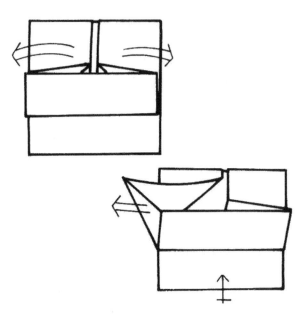

Easy catamaran step 4

Crease-fold where shown to make the middle deck and open the sides, separating to make two hulls. Lower image shows the model upside down; crease along the length of the inner hulls.

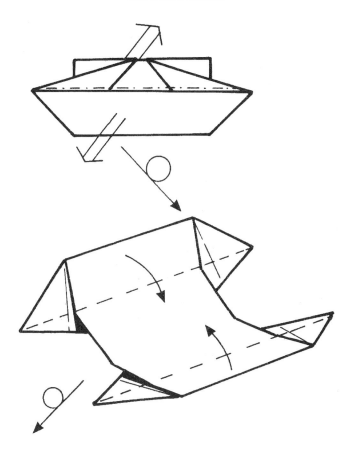

Easy catamaran step 5

The catamaran hull and middle deck is now ready to accept a sail. Steps for the sale are given on the following pages.

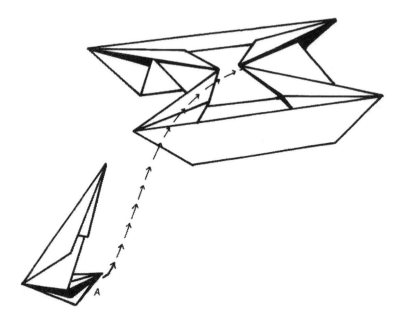

Easy catamaran step 6 – Sail section

Use the cut-off piece of paper (when you made the
square). For the upper two images, fold corners, rotate so
it faces you as indicated for the right-hand image, and
then swing point down diagonally to the left. The bottom
image is the result; fold to the right.

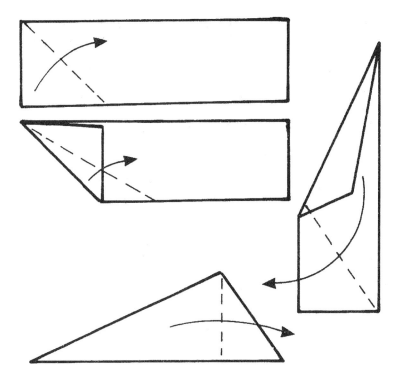

Easy catamaran step 7 – Sail section

Push in at the angle shown and then swing up the sail to a vertical position. This pushed-in section acts as rigidity to keep the sail upright.

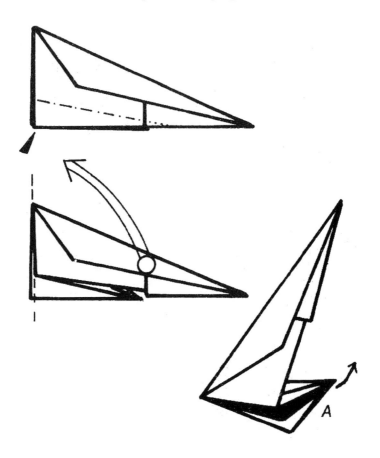

Easy catamaran step 8

Insert the mainsail: slot the small triangle section 'A' into the upper deck section on the catamaran.

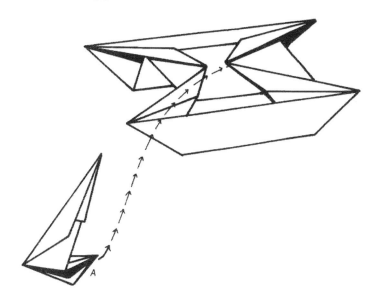

Now we're ready for cat racing!

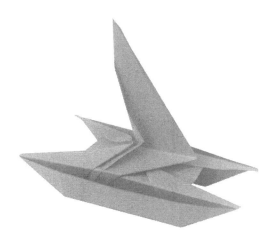

Rich Dude's Cruiser

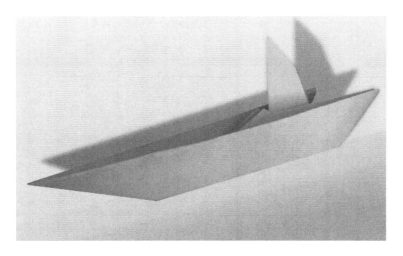

There are a few classy, expensive cruisers moored down at the marina near my place. I once thought about buying a cheap 'do-it-upper' for sale there, but the amount of work involved would have taken me years to complete! At least one can feel like the rich kid on the block with one of these to grace the local ponds and the best thing is: no mooring costs!

Rich dude cruiser Step 1

Begin with a square folded and unfolded diagonally in half, and then fold the sides in to meet the center crease.

(Right-hand image): tuck the small corners underneath and then fold in half.

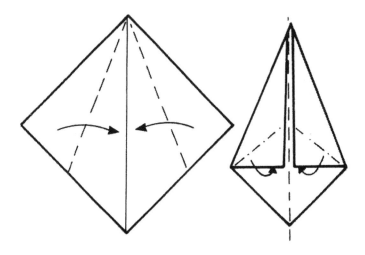

Rich dude cruiser step 2

With the model facing you as shown, crease-well and fold inside and upwards, along the hidden flap edges that are inside.

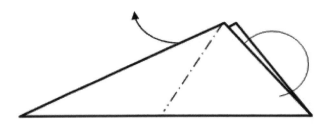

Rich dude cruiser step 3

Crease-fold the hull and then push in the bottom point of the boat's hull. The lower image shows the boat upside-down and how the pushed-in folds are to be made.

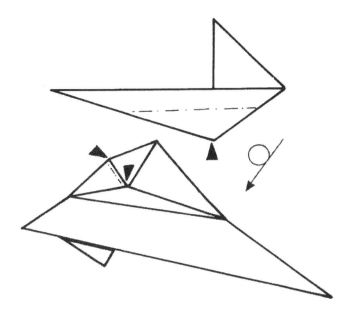

Rich dude cruiser step 4

(Upper image): Invert the 'sail' section, swing it inside and down through the middle of the open-ended hull section.

(Lower image): Open out the stern section by swinging the downward-pointing triangle to the left.

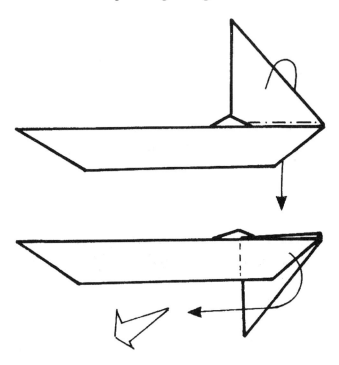

Rich dude cruiser step 5

Close-up of the triangle part of the open section; fold up the flap.

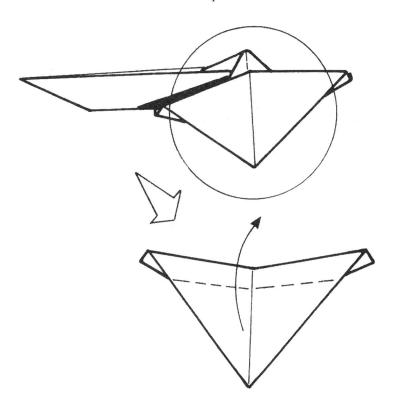

Rich dude cruiser step 6

Place thumb behind area 'A' and fold the flap to the left.
Repeat for the left side and then fold 'B'-'C' back together.

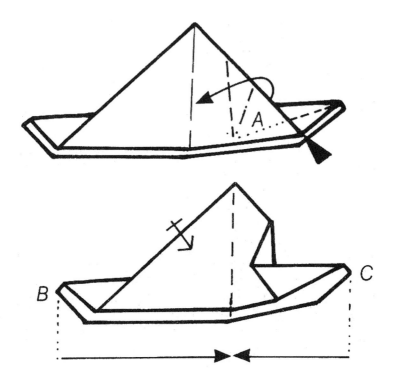

Your rich dude's cruiser is now ready to show off.

Seaplane

If folded using wax paper or other waterproof material, this plane will fly well and glide to a soft water landing, and float thereafter!

Seaplane step 1

Using Letter or A4 paper, make two diagonal creases and a horizontal one folded behind, where the diagonals intersect; and in the bottom right image push the center in and then collapse the sides together.

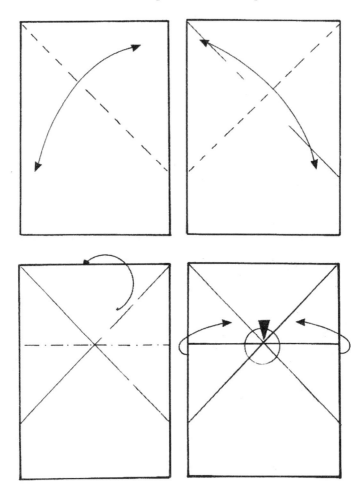

Seaplane step 2

The fold is near-complete; bring all the sides together and flatten the fold.

In the lower image (larger view), crease-fold in the approximate location indicated on both upper flaps.

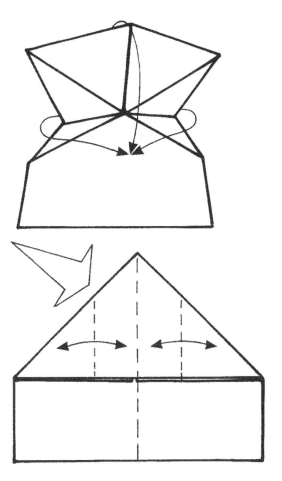

Seaplane step 3

Crease-fold the two corner points and then reverse-fold by placing your finger inside the corners and turning the points inside out, folding back over the edges above. You will need to open out the fold somewhat to make the reverse fold.

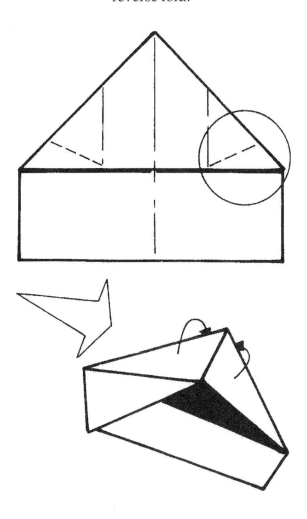

Seaplane step 4

Fold the nose back and then fold in half behind, down the length of the fuselage.

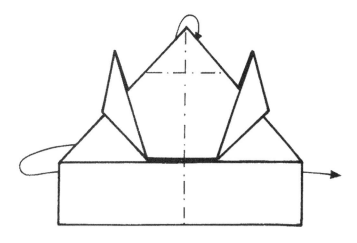

Seaplane step 5

Fold all the trailing edges; tail lift and side fins and then push in the lower right corner, all of which will serve to stop water getting over the wings.

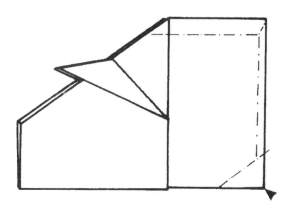

Seaplane step 6

Fold wings down, and then landing skis.

(Lower image): Secure the wing-edge folds made in Step 5 by pushing in the corners and folding the points so they angle snug to the corner. Use tape to secure them if you wish. Some polymers, such as Mylar, is stiff enough not to need tape.

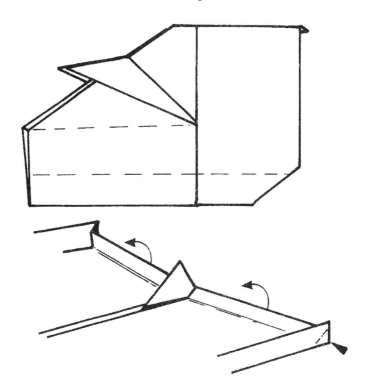

The completed seaplane; open out the water skis with your fingers so that they 'bow' out. This will help your craft stay afloat. Spray with lacquer or vinyl spray paint for waterproofing.

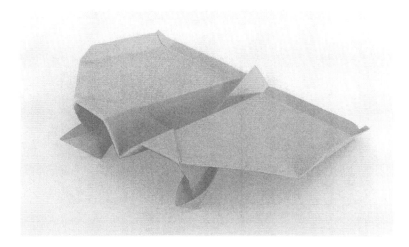

Pirate Ship

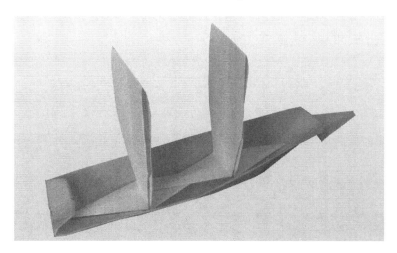

Ahoy there me 'earties; you scurvy lot will have to walk the plank if you can't make this fine vessel! Well that's what Captain Flint says, but if you are like John Silver, you should be able to talk your way out of it!

Pirate ship step 1

Fold a regular sheet of paper in half lengthwise and then fold the corners on each side of the flap that's facing you.

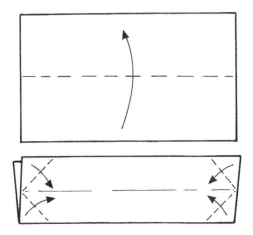

Pirate ship step 2

(Upper image) Fold corners in again and turn over, and (lower image, larger view): fold corners on this side too.

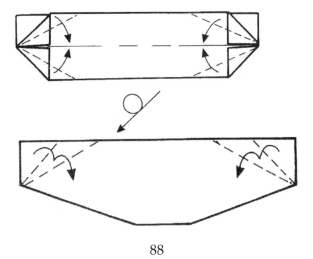

Pirate ship step 3

Fold upper flap down and then crease-fold the bottom of the boat and push in, turning the model to view from the underside, shown in step 4.

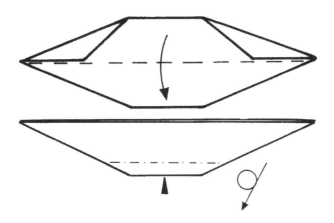

Pirate ship step 4

Flatten the bottom, turn model around and then (lower image) reverse-fold the left section bow, and inverse-fold the right section stern.

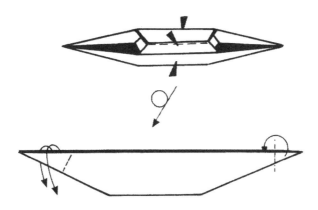

Pirate ship step 5

Fold back the bow to make a nice pointed prow and fold in the stern. Open the model out to look something like that shown in the lower image.

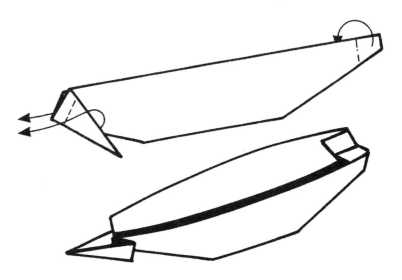

Pirate ship step 6 – sail section

Let's now make some fine sails for our ship. Use black
paper for black sails, if you want. Cut another sheet of A4
or Letter paper lengthwise in half and then cut a half piece
into two quarter strips for our two sails.

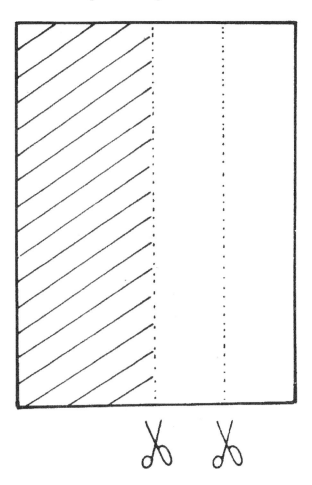

Pirate ship step 7 – sail section

(Upper image): For each sail piece, crease-old in half
vertically and horizontally and then fold in the corners.

(Center image): Fold corners in again so that they overlap.

(Bottom image): Fold in half.

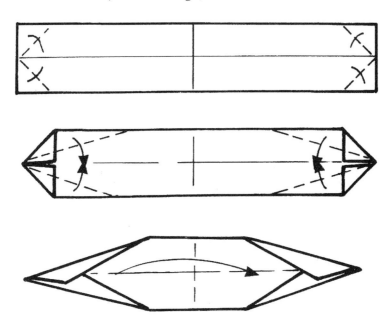

Pirate ship step 8 – sail section

Fold up the points on each side to be at right-angles to the sail. This will be supports for mounting on the hull section.

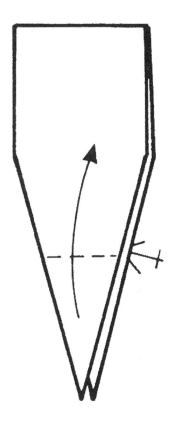

Pirate ship step 9 – sail section

Join the two sail sections together, the center horizontal support points overlapping slightly. Use tape to secure the sails together and then to secure both sails to the boat.

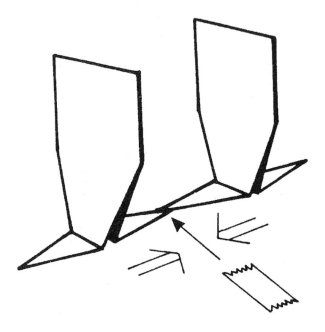

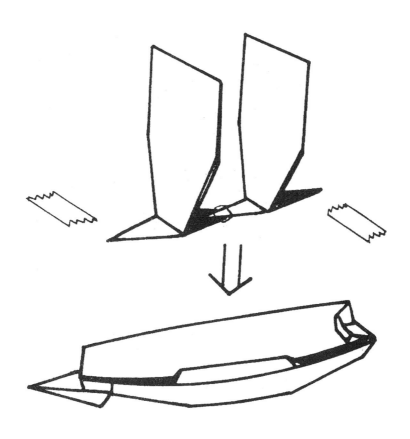

Paint skull and crossbones on the sails and you are now ready to sail the high seas, attack other vessels, rob them of their gold doubloons, force their crew to walk the plank, and all while talking like a pirate, arrgh!

Ocean Liner

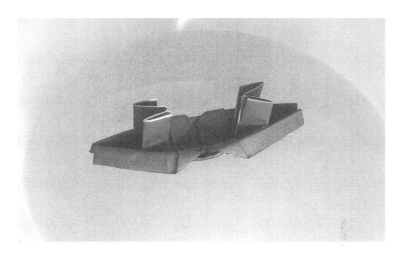

All that talk of pirating and looting may scare you from taking an ocean cruise, but this ship could be tempting. The one shown here is small and floating in a bowl. It's best to build a large one; use a larger piece of paper if you can, such as A3 or a bigger sheet of wax card.

Ocean liner step 1

Cut a sheet of paper in half lengthwise, crease fold the half-piece in half again and then fold edges in to meet the center crease.

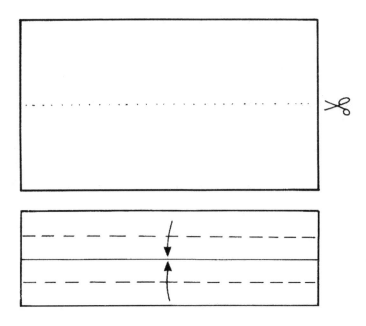

Ocean liner step 2

Fold ends in at one-third intervals, first the left end, and then the right.

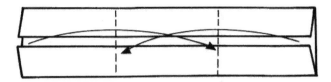

Ocean liner step 3

Fold upper left flap across to the right and then the edge underneath from the right to the left.

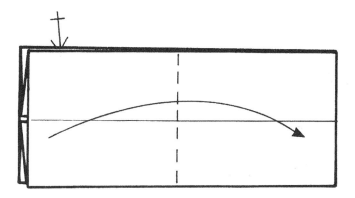

Ocean liner step 4

Fold the upper flaps, outer edges in, squashing the corners flat.

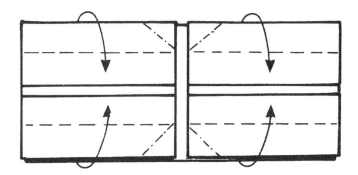

Ocean liner step 5

Fold lengthwise in half.

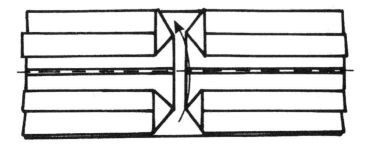

Ocean liner step 6

Lift the inside fold on the left and inverse fold to make the left smoke-stack. The lower image shows the fold nearly done. Repeat for the right stack and then flatten the fold.

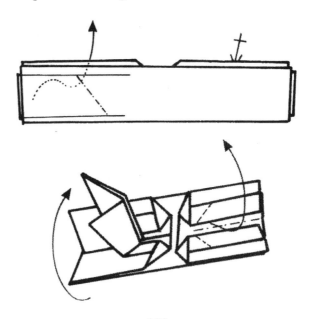

Ocean liner step 7

Smoke stacks done. Fold bow and stern corners in to complete the hull and then fold the horizontal edge down to make the railing, and repeat the railing fold on the other side.

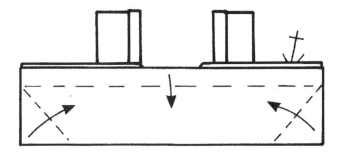

With fingers and thumb gently pull open the boat hull to give it a bowed shape. If the boat tips to one side, crease-fold near the bottom of the hull and push in the section as you did for some of the other boats in this book. This model works best when folded with large paper.

Your completed ocean liner; build a big one for your pool.

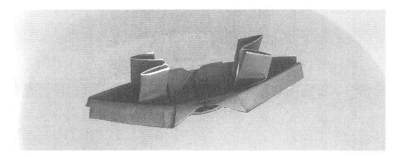

Ballast issues?

Depending on how well you made this craft, you may require some ballast to keep her upright. Weight at the base of the hull is recommended, such as a paper clip or coin. If you make a larger vessel, try sticking a pen along the base of the hull for horizontal ballast. Our little ship in the bowl floats well without any added ballast.

Aircraft Carrier

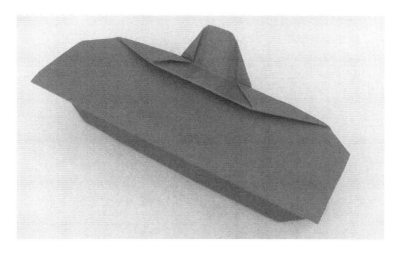

This is a tricky one in that you need to fold it correctly in order to have it float. Once mastered, you can have a lot of fun trying to land your paper airplanes on a big aircraft carrier in your swimming pool :) and if you do have ballast issues, there is a way to improve it without adding any extra weight!

Aircraft carrier step 1

Use a really big piece of paper or card. Cut the long edge off so that the aspect ratio is a longer rectangle. Now fold in half.

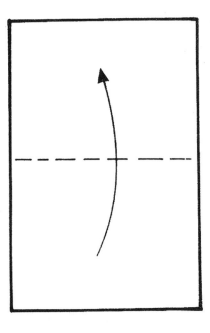

Aircraft carrier step 2

Measure and inch and a half (approx. 4cm) from the
bottom folded edge, crease fold and inverse the corners
diagonally, and then fold down the flaps along the crease.

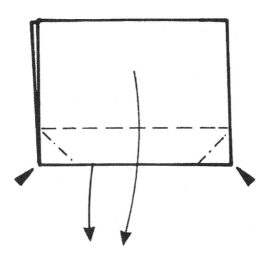

Aircraft carrier step 3

Swing the flap behind back up and then fold its corners in diagonally.

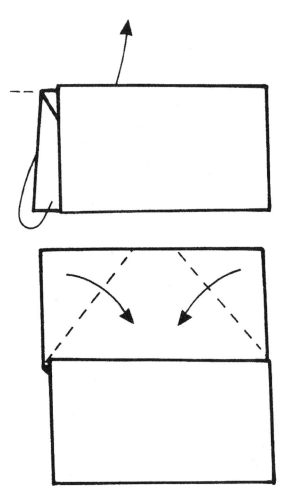

Aircraft carrier step 4

Still on the same flap, fold top point down and then back up along the dashes. This flap will become the flight 'control tower'.

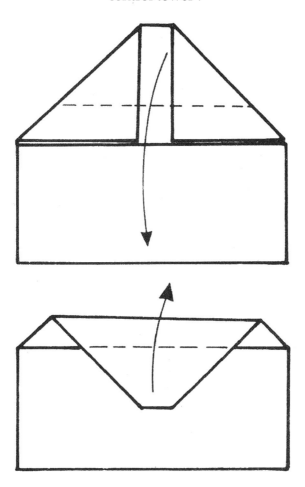

Aircraft carrier step 5

Tuck fingers behind the flaps, pull towards the center and flatten.

(Lower image): Crease-fold along *xx* and *yy* and tuck under the flight control tower's long edge.

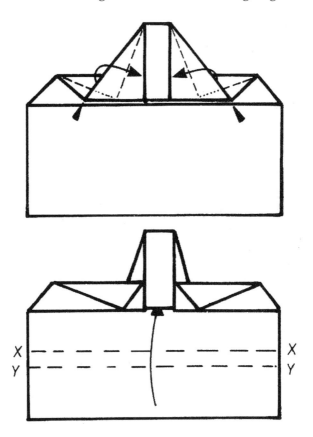

Aircraft carrier step 6

(Upper image): Fold up the control tower section.

(Lower image): Open the hull to create a new fold as shown in *xx*. This will create a wider hull in which to create ballast (which can be a heavy pen, drill bit, line of coins etc.). Tape the flight control tower section to the flight deck to secure the fold. Fold corners A and B behind to secure the hull.

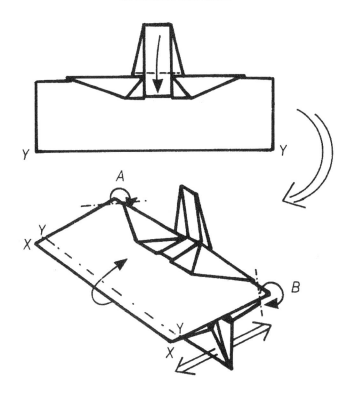

If you want a floating craft without needing added weight, try these steps…

Aircraft carrier step 7 – hull modification

Turn your model upside down and crease-fold well the hull section. We will push this section in as we have done for other boats in this book. Crease well.

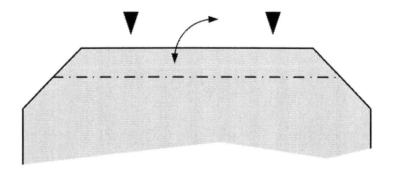

Aircraft carrier step 8 – hull modification

Open out your model and push inwards along the bottom
of the hull.

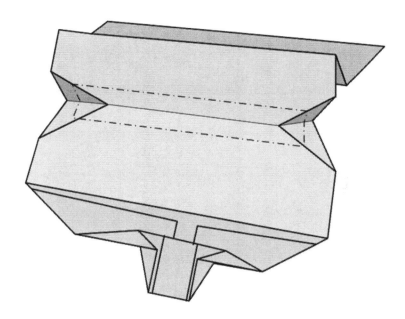

Aircraft carrier step 9 – hull modification

Collapse in the pushed-in fold on each end and it will look like the left image. Push in the corners to reinforce the hull.

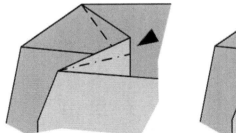 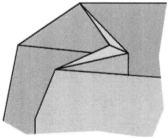

Here is a close-up photo of the modified underside.

And you are done! Bring the ship together again, noting step 6.

Your completed aircraft carrier; if you want to use even larger sheets of paper or card (or waterproof card), ensure the folds are well-creased. Use spray lacquer to help waterproof your craft, and for a fun competition, try and land your paper aircraft on it.

About the Author

Carmel Duryea Morris is a multi-talented designer and writer of some 35 books for children, her first book published when she was a teenager. These consist of 3D graphics art books, fiction (*Cod Almighty*, *Forest of the Last*) and origami books such as *Fold Your Own Dinosaurs* and *Fold Your Own Bugs*. Her *Best Advanced Paper Aircraft* series have sold hundreds of thousands of copies worldwide and were featured in WIRED magazine. She has appeared on *The Late Show* in LA and has lectured at several universities on flight theory, teaching many young and old how to master paper aircraft building for fun, education, competitions and stress relief!

A music composer, she also has an album released and available on iTunes, *Another Number*, and has contributed to various record label theme albums, including her re-work of the James Bond theme, *The Living Daylights* (also available on iTunes).

She is a software designer working for a well-regarded audio engineering laboratory, technical writer, sci-fi lover and ham radio nut. In the innovative family tradition of her ancestor, Charles Duryea (Duryea Motor Corporation), she also converted an old two door sports coupe into an all-electric vehicle, using lithium phosphate batteries. She now drives happily around town without spending a dime on gas.

29546535R00066

Printed in Great Britain
by Amazon